# PURPLE KISSES

Poems
By
Nadine Fagan
a.k.a
"Nana"

**SEASON#1**

ISBN: 978-0-578-85144-0

Printed by Power Of Purpose Publishing www.PopPublishing.com Atlanta, Ga. 30326

Philippians 4:13

"I can do all things through him
and who strengthens me"

# AUTHOR BIO

I recall every Sunday, there I was, cutting out the poetry section from the Gleaner; our local newspaper in Jamaica, at that time when growing up on the island. Poetry has not only been a long time passion of mine, but was also an outlet of expressing myself as I had a speech impediment as a child. So when I wasn't cutting the Sunday paper, I was writing my poems on any piece of paper I could find, until I was afforded a small note book, that I have to this day. I believe I have had a somewhat blessed life thus far. I have had some hardships, some struggles, times when I just wanted to end it all, before marriage and after marriage adversities, and through all that, my writing was my therapy, then led to my performing at various open-mic spots in the city, at different events, in the US, Canada and Jamaica. Writing helped me through my healing process, made me find myself discovering who I am, how important self-care is, what love and nurturing oneself means. I truly have much to be grateful for, and give thanks that I have the ability to leave behind something more than material things, more than money, something for my children that is worth more than silver and gold. That's when I decided that my greatest gift to my children would be this book of poetries, authentically me, sharing words of wisdom, inspiration, motivation, courage and strength, with hopes that this book will be an example of; "I can do anything", and that the sky is not the limit.

I've accomplished so much in my life such as; migrating from Kingston, Jamaica to Toronto, Canada, the school choir, to track star, who made it to the OFSAA Athletic book of records, breaking the long jump record for all of Toronto in 1989. To hip hop, break dancing, battling against the best of the best on the dance floor, both male and female, to forming my own dance group "Spicy Six", we performed in different events and took part in talent shows hosted by Jones and Jones Production. It was an honor to have blessed the stage with other artists like KRS-1, Public Enemy, Mc Lyte, Heavy D (R.I.P), Queen Latifa, Monie Love, etc. From there I began working on set of two of Canada's most popular urban T.V series, My Secret Identity and Drop the Beat. I since then have achieved my nursing degree, while I've done it all while facing many challenges but knew that something greater would come one day. Hence the collection of my poems being curated into a book. This book is a compilation of poems that I have written throughout the years that will hopefully inspire you as much as they have inspired me. Welcome to my journey.


Welcome to my journey.

# ACKNOWLEDGMENTS

First I need to thank my Lord and Savior for granting me the serenity and humbleness gained during this journey. Thank you my three heartbeats; Ty, Tre, and Terri, and this I say; my legacy to you three. Thank you to everyone who has ever contributed to this journey, everyone who believed in my vision, everyone who believed in me…

Thank You!

# CONTENTS

# PURPLE KISSES

# TEMPLE

They say the body and or your body is your TEMPLE, but yet still it has a reputation of being violated by the "somewhat" God's gift to women…

My TEMPLE is constantly misused, abused, neglected, jeopardized and told nothing but lies, when I or you let the shit happen…

How do you stop the invaders when you let your guard down with a frown, when you disapprove and yet he still pursues, she cries rape, he says it's a mistake; "she wanted it", did u see the way she was dressed!?...Yes she is a sistah of many colors, the fruit of nature, but u, u manipulator, trespasser, violator! Who gives you the right to put it there, when you were not invited into the ocean of natural fruit juices of life?

All you did was contaminate while you penetrate, causing so much hurtful pleasure and deep thrusting pain, that only leaves reflections that can't be erased…

P.S.

A TEMPLE is a holy place for worship and prayers…

# LOST

I am LOST in my memories, stuck in my thoughts…I'm supposedly on vacation, but got caught in an Amazon of lust, infatuation and lies…

Do I end my vacation? My trip away from time or do I commit a crime that will give me peace of mind…

I am insane with pain cause they all the same, play with your buttons like you are made from cotton…

You let them touch it, sniff it, taste it, then abuse it with hard deep wet pain, when my tongue spoke juicy sweet lyrics on your manhood….haha, that made you smile, you cried out in agony, while I lay in my thoughts…wondering, "did I get caught?"

# YOU

"Not YOU too,"YOU suppose to be my lion from Zion, but no man is an island, and yet sistahs are treated like an exotic vacation spot…when YOU think, aahh its time to take a vacation, from one sistah to another, then another…till death do us part!

"Not YOU too", YOU a hustler, I am a sufferer…suffering from the undying affection and love that I need for my body, mind and soul, "NO" not my hole…it's always misunderstood when a sistah requests love or affection, it's often interrupted as; "that sistah needs a "FUCK!!" Oh we got such luck…

"Not YOU too," YOU know any brotha that offers affection, love and attention? Maybe even a little compassion, relaxation; without not trying to get between a sistahs thighs, to touch her hot wet pie, while he thinks…should I have some pie and make her cry? Or left to die?

"Not YOU Too!!"

# "LION"

Is it real or just one of them things…would it be that I've found my real Lion, hey the one from Zion or could it be a trespasser who has plans for my treasure, will he roar the right words that a vulnerable sistah wants to hear…

Just to be loved and feel loved or will he just dive in and take a swim into my deep ocean of love or as they call it; the pleasa, the teasa, the headache easa…

As he caresses my thoughts with his prerogative words, I got lost in myself; the words he spoke were so tame, like his lustrous mane…

Stimulating fuljoyment from the lion's superior anatomy left my nature throbbing with anxiety, of course it wasn't right but who's to say it was wrong…it should have been just a mere infatuation, but instead it was a lot of penetration that led me to frustration

Is this my Lion? Could he be from Zion?!!

# OVERDRIVE

My thoughts are in overdrive, yet I find words to put on paper….all I'm trying to do is hold back tears wondering; apart from my three heartbeats (my children), who the hell loves me?...

My intelligence is constantly being trampled on…I'm known as; "Miss know it all", and always been talked down too, so I can feel belittled…

I am not wanted in this sanctuary anymore, the money is done, it's time to go back to my miserable life that only brings me pain and frustration, should I be here, here on earth when all you ask for or try to gain in life is happiness? Yes my children bring me happiness, but there is just something missing, I need peace of mind, they say you can't run from your troubles, I think; silly me try to do that…and it's just not happening. I ask the good God almighty for guidance, but maybe too blind to see, to see beyond my miserable thoughts, thoughts that are now in overdrive…

How do I slow it down, should I stay on the freeway or take the back roads, maybe just continue until I run out of gas…This all sounds like I'm starting to drown in my own ocean, the ocean of self pity! When will I be rescued or will I ever be rescued, rescued from myself…

I wish you long life and prosperity they say when you think you are alone in the world with your pain and sorrows, there is always someone else with a situation worse than yours….(sigh) Just breathe out negativity and inhale positivity, and that should help you get by with a little serenity…

# "DAY DREAMS"

Today is not yet determined, but I made it through the day by giving thanks to the almighty for health, strength, liberation, independence, freedom…the freedom to speak, freedom to touch and be touched, to love and be loved, the freedom to be, taking back your right, your right to be a woman of dignity, pride and substance…yeh! Well that will be for today because tomorrow will come and my memories will have me somewhat impaired, that I will not be able to walk a straight line if my life depended on it

But what is it I/you seek? Peace? Tranquility?...everlasting love, is it out there? Such an easy uttering request, will I wake from my captivating dreams into this miserable reality, my reality of self pity, pity that only I, myself and I can withdraw myself from…how do you do that? Many wonder, but seemingly without a doubt, I/you just want the courage to be oneself…

I think you/we must live for today and fuck what might come tomorrow….Live Laugh Love

# RELATION

I have found the words, but too afraid they might come out the wrong way, where do I start? At the end, the beginning or the middle? Do I tell you and not fear how much pain you will feel due to the pain that I have felt, am feeling or do I just be that outspoken bitch I have always been?…

Do I say love is not just materialized, symbolic or fucking…do I tell you it won't work because you don't put in the work, the dedication, the time, the attention, the togetherness?

Don't you remember your first love? Why can't it be like that, what happened to all that warmth? Maybe you are not trying, but can you try just a little bit harder, a little passion, some romance, a little laughter, a few games or is it too late? Can't teach an old dog new tricks, because you have led me to fall out of, what I thought was…love, too many lies, too many cries, too many friends, hanging on the ends…

# HAPPY

When it's said; I could have, I want too, I will, I can, make you happy…do they know what an empress like I or you require when the above statement is used and misused over and over again?

Each sistah has their own concept on "happy", some sistahs think having the most expensive name brand items is happiness, while others think; being in a "FUCK ME WHEN YOUR GIRL IS ON HER MONTHLY" relationship with another sistahs man makes her happy…

For me, the simplest things in life makes me happy, I guess I'm just a naturalist from birth…he said I could have made you happy, he speaks in the past…would I have been happy when our eyes made four? Or would he have held out and make me continue to feel lost, trapped in my thoughts, thoughts of needing and wanting happiness, not just the mere happiness from back to back orgasmic explosions that subsides from every nerve in my lifeless body jonesing, feening for more like a drug addict going through detox…God's gift to the Goddesses of this race, yeh you know that special place in between that space, that when all else fails, you know you have guaranteed happiness just arms length away, that gives you pleasure and not pain…when flicked, licked and caressed the right way…you can easily draw for them triple "A's"…I never run out of them, shiiiit….pass me a spliff!

# WHY

Why can't you love only me instead of sniffing every ass you see like some little puppy trying to find himself a bone?

Why can't you be there for me when I'm going through my emotions, the surface from my ocean?

Why can't you be home on time, instead of committing a crime, that includes infidelity and lies?…you should be home when I get there, with meals prepared, my bath running and my favorite jam pumping…

Do you know my favorite jams, my favorite flicks, what makes me thick and that it's you that makes me sick…will you ever know me or just my pussy that brings you to your ecstasy

What do you want from me…my loving or my cumming, let me guess, nevertheless, it's a mess…why do you make me cry, do you feel satisfied when you lie

Why can't you love me for me, and cherish the very ground that echoes with pain from my every step…is it because you are of many colors, like the lizard you are…bore you some fruits of which should multiply, I am just your concubine with no love inclined?

Why?

Will I be loved by you when I decide, we are through? I think it's too late…don't even bother to compensate

# THE LINK

FOREVER AND FOR ALWAYS ARE WORDS I SPEAK, A CHAIN IS AS STRONG AS ITS WEAKEST LINK, THAT LINK I DARE NOT BE...

I AM THE LINK OF ETERNITY, THE LEADER THAT WILL ALWAYS BE, GIVE ME A CHANCE AND YOU WILL SEE, THAT YOUR BEST FRIEND CAN BE YOUR WORST ENEMY, THOSE LINKS ARE CALLED; "FRIEND ENEMY"...

YES, THAT COULD BE ME, YOU, HE OR SHE...WITH THE ANGEL SMILE, BUT THE DEVIL FROM THE PILE, FILLED WITH LIES, TRUST ME MAN, and YOU KNOW I UNDERSTAND...

FILL THEM WITH YOUR DEEPEST, SWEETEST FAIRY TALES THAT COULD SEND YOU TO JAIL, WHAT DOES THIS ENTAIL, A LINK YOU THOUGHT WOULD HAVE NEVER FAILED...

FOREVER AND FOR ALWAYS ARE THE WORDS THE BROTHAS SPEAK, THEY WILL FOREVER HAVE A CHAIN OF FOOLS WHICH IS WHERE I DARE NOT BE, YOU SEE US SISTAHS, WHETHER YOU A MOTHER, SISTER, COUSIN OR A NIECE, WE ALL NEED TO GET SOME PEACE. WE ALL A VICTIM OF THE BROTHA'S CHAIN OF FOOLS, BUT HEY; DID THEY KNOW THIS IS THE NEW SKOOL...BROTHAS HAVE TAUGHT US SO WELL, NOW WE THE TEACHERS IN THIS HELL

CHAIN OF FOOLS, WHO MADE THE RULES, WHY THEY THINK ALL LINKS IN THEIR CHAIN WILL REMAIN THE SAME…NO I REFUSE TO BE TAME, SLIGHTLY INSANE…BROTHAS YOU NEED TO BE TAME, FOR WE WILL NO LONGER ACCEPT THE LAST NAME…

# KICKING IT…

WHAT TO TALK ABOUT TODAY; DO I LEAVE OR DO I STAY, DO I SWALLOW OR REGURGITATE, DO I CUM OR DO I FAKE?…

AM I HIGH OR JUST IMPAIRED FROM MY SIGH, IS IT THE CALIWEED OR JUST SOME NATURAL VIBEZ?…

WHAT LEADS ME TO MY LYRICS OF EXPLICITS, DO I RHYME ON TIME WITH MY STATE OF MIND, AM I INTOXICATED WITH LUST, SHOULD I FUSS OR IS IT A PLUS BECAUSE I MUST?…

IT'S A MUST THAT YOU BE FREE, FREE IN MIND, BODY AND SOUL…ARE YOU UP FOR THE CHALLENGE, ARE YOU UP FOR SOME MORE, MORE SENSUOUS LYRICS THAT I MOAN WHEN I CUM, DO YOU WANT TO DEVOUR ME AS MAIN COURSE OR WOULD YOU RATHER HAVE ME AT YOUR LEISURE WITH RHYTHMIC PLEASURE?…

AM I SATISFYING THE MIND, DO I SEEM DIVINE….AM I LYRICALLY INCLINED, WILL YOU BE MINE…FROM TIME TO TIME??

# EMPRESS

THEY CAN'T KEEP A GOOD WOMAN DOWN….ALL THEY TRY
I AIN'T GONNA FROWN…THEY CAN NEVER, NEVER TAKE I
FOR A CLOWN…

EVERYWHERE IN THE WORLD THERE IS DESTRUCTION
AND PAIN…YOU TRY TO BUILD A FAMILY AND WHAT IS IT
YOU GAIN…. ANIMOSITY, ENVY AND FRAUD FAME…. A SO
CALLED LOVE YOU WAIT FOR IN VAIN…

FRIENDS DECEIVE YOU FOR YOUR STRUGGLE TO GAIN
THE FAME, NOT KNOWING THAT HEARTACHE IS WORSE
THAN LABOR PAIN…

NEVER AGAIN, ONCE MORE I SIGH, LIFT UP YOUR HEADS,
STRONG SISTAH NOH CRY…I AM A EMPRESS OF THE
MOST HIGH, BUT WHAT DO I DO WHEN I COME TO MY LAST
SIGH? JUST HOLD MY HEAD HIGH AND PRAISE JAH
RASTAFARI…

BLACK EMPRESS COMES FIRST, AND THAT IS I…

# Living A Dream…

I HAVE SUBDUED MYSELF IN MY THOUGHTS, REMINISCING ON WHAT WAS, AND WHAT COULD HAVE BEEN…

CONSOLED ME WITH HIS UNDIVIDED TOUCH AND EMBRACE, COULD I HAVE LOST IT ALL BEFORE IT HAS FALLEN IN PLACE…

THERE IS ONLY ONE THING ON MY MIND…I'M READY TO HOLD YOU, LOVE YOU AND ENGULF YOU WITH LOVE NEVER ENDING, EVEN WHEN WE HAVE GONE TO THE UNDERWORLD OUR LOVE WILL STILL LINGER LIKE THE LOVE A MOTHER HAS FOR HER CHILD…

I AM IN LOVE, WANT LOVE, NEED LOVE, HAVE LOVE FOR YOU, HOW ELSE CAN I EXPRESS IT…MY WORDS ARE DEEP, SO TAKE HEED!...

# CONVENIENCE

HERE IS WHAT HE TOLD ME; he said he went to the convenience store the other day…

Said he bought two smiles, ten giggles, three hugs and one, I will call you later…

However, while in the convenience store, he said he tripped and fell on me that is, I pondered on the mere fact that I was only a convenience store and he was only visiting, which in reality was we sistahs were sometimes being used for convenient purposes to satisfy his/their everyday pleasures…

This has somewhat been going on for many years now, but you can also call it lifetime events that sistahs everywhere in the world let happen…

He said he also picked up a few pipe cleaners, a couple of guns, a possible HIV and maybe a few kids here and there, that he knows nothing of, or just in denial, denying that these stories were becoming too convenient for his demeaning lifestyle…

He then decided to purchase a convenient store for his everyday needs, yet that still wasn't enough…

He said there were items that his store did not provide, he wanted it all, butt washing, butt fucking, then shit happens…

It was too late, his store closed down, and so did he…

# D.I.E

(Death Is Eternal)
For My 3HeartBeats...


If I die, when I die, will my children remember me by, will they always cry, wondering why, why did mommy die...

If I die, when I die, will my children get a piece of the pie... will they be loved and cherished like I did before I perished, will they be taught to love and live without me, and taught the values of life before it has begun, knowing that life goes on...

If I die, when I die, will my babies know why, will they say goodbye or just have a long sigh...will their memories be filled with joy before mommy died...

If I die, when I die, will they know their mother's love was unconditional, will they remember me, and not the material...?

Ty, Terri and Tre, always remember to pray, love and take care of each other, and don't forget your father...

Remember I will always be there, so never despair...love you always and forever, and that's my sincere promise...

# FREE

You tell me you love me, yet your friends come first…you leave me at nights longing to quench my thirst

I need to know who comes first, is it us or is that too much, too much for you to live the life called; husband and wife

Do you know the meaning of "husband', do you know its repertoire…you are so timid that our relationship has gotten frigid…

Why don't you let me be, so you can be free, as it seems you are already free, free from me…

# LET GO

Love it or leave it, Let go...that what they say, but how can you give all that love, then walk away...I was blind, looking through the eyes of others, then took a good look inside myself, seeing what matters...I was lethargic at first, but time heals all wounds...drowning in self-pity and sorrow, no more; because I have let go and swam to the safety shore, far from the deep end I dare not explore, there ain't nothing that can phase me, for that I am sure...

Letting go...I am beatific, and loving it, peaceful and jovial...they ask; how will you do it, he named you, claimed you...they are so yesterday, so mundane...I am human, not insane...

# BLESSED

Life has in sighted me on how brilliantly blessed we are, how beautiful we are inside and out, our individual strengths and weaknesses, weaknesses we somehow give ourselves…to realize that we have somehow overcome weakness, we must first be strong, strong as a sistah or brother in this devil hell society, the society that says we are invisible and tries to break us down…

I am wonderful, marvelous, fabulous, no one can control us, hold us, mold us…they can try to console us, but did they know that we are malcontent, do these devils know we are more fas-tid-i-ous or is that just a bit too ridiculous…we shouldn't have a mind of our own, speak only when spoken too, if they want an opinion they will give us one…

No not today, maybe yesterday…as we are so blessed, no stress, here to set examples, strive and change lives…So everybody high five!

# "INTRUDER"

It was just like a mystery movie, keeping you on the edge of your seat wondering what's next, should you move, can I go to the bathroom, get more popcorn, a glass of wine, red preferably, smooth, sweet…you see my man was all over me on the dance floor, but for some strange reason I felt it was a show, cause she stared and she stared, she stared with that astonished look on her, somewhat cute face, she kinda looked like me, like his type, but she wasn't as cute as me, as fine or as blessed asI am…

I love my man, and my man loves me, only me…

The mystery got more intense, girlfriend stepped up to my man and demanded that he step away from me, I held him tighter…then thought; should I swing or leave it up to him…would he do the right thing, would he know who comes first, quench my thirst?…

# SWEET

I wanted to say something, something short and sweet, something to tickle your feet…something to give you some heat…

Wait! Just let me speak, I'm gonna say something sweet…but when can we meet, I wanna give you a treat, a treat that will leave your whole body agonized with pleasure, so tantalized you might be left paralyzed…

But wait! This is what I realized, I need you, I want you…but do you feel me though...

You so sweet, you make me think of the ice cream parlor I went to last week, imma be your vanilla and you, all the toppings that me your vanilla can endure…we can start with fudge and end with cherries, I'll be left wanting, more and more…I wanna take you to my heaven, your whole persona, your tone a soft whisper that makes me shiver…

I'm not quite finished yet, but imma wait till I see ya!

# FRUIT

It was a day in July, I was drunk, nervous, scared, weak, but strong black, a strong black sistah who thought about setting the perfect example to other sistahs and brothers who thought it couldn't happen, it won't happen it won't work, they are not ready, ready for that challenge in life they call husband and wife...

I was ready, been ready, my fruit was ripe and ready to be picked with the soft tender hands of life, caressed with laughter, whispers, maybe a little roughness, even a playful bite...but no, this fruit must be handled with care, for this fruit is very fragile, versatile, yes a little spoiled...

I am benignly known for my kindly tone, others find malignant to their souls....

# "TRULY DEEP"

IT'S TRULY A BLESSING TO SEE US CONGREGATE IN THIS LITTLE HAVEN, THEY CALL IT; PLANTATION…

PLANTATION! THIS REMINDS ME OF OUR FOREMOTHERS, FATHERS, BROTHERS, SISTERS, AND THE LIST GOES ON….AS THEY ANSWER TOO: YES MASTER (YES MASAH), NO MASTER (NO MASAH)…MASTERS THAT MADE THEM SLAVES, WHICH LED THEM TO THEIR GRAVES…

IT'S TRULY A BLESSING TO SEE US COME TOGETHER AS ONE, AND THEM AS NONE, PAVING THE WAY FOR OUR NEW GENERATION…

OH PLANTATION! THIS IS THE NATION OF TODAY AND TOMORROW, THE NATION THAT IS UNSTOPPABLE; UNTOUCHABLE…WE ARE SO GIFTED, WONDERFULLY BLESSED. WE ARE THE ROSA PARKS OF TODAY, SHE MIGHT HAVE SAT A SEAT FROM THE DRIVER, BUT WE IN THE FRONT SEAT, THE DRIVER'S SEAT, DRIVING TO NEVER TURNING BACK, TO THE BROTHERS AND SISTERS WHO HAVE GOT CAUGHT UP IN THE WEB THAT HAS SOMEHOW BLURRED THEIR VISION, THE VISION TO THEIR IDENTITY…CAN'T YOU SEE THEY ARE TRYING TO TAKE OUR BROTHERS AND SISTERS AWAY THEY ARE TRYING TO DO US, BE US, LOOK LIKE US…THEY GO IN MACHINES TO GET OUR SKIN, OUR TONE OUR WHOLE PERSONA…DON'T THEY KNOW OUR BEAUTY IS SKIN DEEP…

LET FREEDOM REIGN, ARE THE WORDS, THE MESSAGE FROM OUR LEADERS BEFORE US, OVER US, INSIDE US…WE ARE TRULY BLESSED, WE KNOW THE RIGHT THING, SO DO THE RIGHT THING…

WAKE UP AND SMELL THE COFFEE IS A JARGON OF THEIR NATION…

TODAY'S NATIONS ARE THE LEADERS IN THIS "PLANTATION" LEADING US TO A WHOLE NEW GENERATION…

# DIVINE

Divine love is doing its perfect work in, through, for and round about me now…

Divine love goes before me making easy and prosperous my way…

Divine love has lustrously lubricated my fruitful pleasure…some call it the teasa, tickla, the headache pleasa!

Divine love have has led me into temptation, divine love has left my nipples protruding and his nature was ruling every inch of my oven, a fire has ignited…I just can't fight it, I'm gonna need an extinguisher, cause boy you light my fire…you my every desire…

Divine love has turned me into a feen Queen, but could it be my self esteem…Bombs exploding, no fire work that can explain this Divine love on mother earth…The forecast called for showers, showers of passionate love making, but forgot to mention the flooding down south, life jackets will be an asset , never forget it!

As Divine as I am; the feen Queen, the mental stimulation being…will leave you feening, believe me you will be steaming…

# LAST NITE

IT'S MORNING AND NOW IT'S TIME FOR US TO START
AGAIN....YES BABY, IT HAPPENED AND I DIDN'T GET
ENOUGH LAST NITE...YES WE'VE STOLEN THAT MOMENT
NOW IT'S TIME FOR US TO START AGAIN...

MY BODY YEARNING LKE A CELIBATE CAT IN HEAT...HAS
THE BEATING OF MY HEART PULSATED BETWEEN MY
THIGHS, WITH EVERY BREATH I TAKE,WHEN I REMINICE
ON HOW HE ENGULFED ME LAST NITE...I GET WEAK, WET,
HELPLESS, SPEECHLESS....OH LAST NITE!

# HEAVEN

Heaven! Is it heaven on earth or heaven under the earth, is it when you have said your last goodbyes or when it's down to your last sigh…Is there really another side or you're just left to wonder why, when, where, how?

Where do you go after you've died? Some say heaven, some say hell…how will it be determined, what's your destination, they say trust in the Lord for with him you will have a perfect relation…he will direct you to his peaceful haven, where you will have peace from this earth and everlasting blessings…

Heaven to me is; death…when you've spoken your last breath, and hell is what we are today, how we pray, how we strive, which way to survive…how to stay alive, what to do to get by, when will we die...all the tears you have cried, hell is living in misery, condemning each other for we are no blood brothers…in the eyes of the Lord he sees us as one, he scripted commandments for which we are to follow, and in return he shows us the light through the tunnel, tunnel to peace, serenity, eternal life…

It's left up to us to make the decision, as we all have our own destination for a life in heaven or hell…Just take heed and look within yourself, for only you can tell if it's heaven or hell…

# ONLY IF

HIS SILHOUETTE STILL LINGERS AS I TRY TO CARRY ON, WHO COULD FORGET THE WARMTH OF HIS CHARM, HIS TASTEFUL SMILE THAT LASTED A WHILE, THE WAY HE LOOKED AT ME MADE ME SHIVER, WHEN HE TOUCHED ME I MELTED INTO A RIVER, HIS AURA MADE ME INTO AN EXPLORER OF THE HUMAN RACE, OPPOSITE TO MY FACE.....OH AMAZING GRACE!

HOW I'M LONGING TO SEE HIS FACE , HIS TASTE, BECOME ONE WITH HIM, I WANT TO GET INSIDE HIS MIND BODY AND SOUL, I WANT TO CONSOLE HIM, MOLD HIM...I TOLD HIM ABOUT MY DREAM MY WET DREAMS, MY EVERY NEED, MY DILDOS AND MY FRIENDLY HELLOS FROM THOSE MANLY HOES, ONLY HEAVEN KNOWS...HOW MY BODY YEARNS FOR HIS THRUSTING BURNS, WILL HE EVER LEARN WHAT HIS LOOK, HIS TOUCH, HIS TASTE, HIS FEEL, HIS WHOLE APPEAL HAS DONE TO ME, ON A REAL....ONLY IF!

# "THINK"

I have been a little under the weather, jonesing for some tasty pleasure, who would have known I would have to face a little measure…

I am a bit optimistic, due to my vital statistic, who you think you messing with, do you think I am pessimistic, would you like me to elaborate or compensate for your time?…You seem to be lyrically inclined, in my mind do not enter the sign, u might get it twisted and lose your mind…

So take heed to this message, even if it's kinda twisted, but should you figure it out, then you should be proud…

# BLACK

BLACK IS THE ESSENCE OF WHO I AM, IT'S WHAT MADE ME SO STRONG, NOT AS A MAN, BUT AS BLACK WOMAN WITH A BACKBONE OF YESTERDAY, TODAY AND TOMORROW…

I AM THE ESSENCE OF EVERYTHING BLACK, MY WAYS, MY MEANS, MY WHOLE BEING…LOOK DEEP INSIDE YOURSELF, and YOU WILL SEE WHAT I MEAN…

BLACK IS BEAUTIFUL AND JOVIAL, BLACK IS NOT ONLY THE COLOR OF MY SKIN, IT'S DEEP WITHIN, IT'S IN EVERY FOLLICLE OF MY HAIR, IN MY EYES, IN MY SMILES, EVEN IN THE CLOTHES I WEAR…NO NEED TO COMPARE, TO HAVE THAT STRAIGHT HAIR, TO LIGHTEN THE SKIN FOR THAT WHITISH TINT…

BLACK IS EVERYTHING PURE, FOR SURE, LOVED AND ADORED…BUT YOU SEE, WE HAVE BEEN ENVIED, HATED, BEEN EMANCIPATED, YET CONDITIONED TO EMULATE A RACE THAT HAS NO PLACE…UNKNOWN FILLED WITH CLONES, I KNOW I AINT ALONE…RESEARCHING THE MELANIN IN MY SKIN, PRODUCING THINGS THAT HAS NO MEANING…

BLACK SO BEAUTIFUL….BLACK SO PURE, DO I NEED TO SAY MORE!

# COLD

IT WAS A VERY COLD NIGHT LAST-NIGHT, HE WAS THERE...BUT I DIDN'T FEEL HIS WARMTH, HE WAS SUBDUED IN HIS THOUGHTS THAT HE FORGOT THAT HIS EMPRESS WAITS TO ENTER THE DOOR TO HIS TEMPLE...

IT WAS AN OCCASIONAL GLANCE, AN OCCASIONAL HOW YOU DOING, BUT HE DIDN'T KNOW I NEEDED TO FEEL HIS EMBRACE, HIS HANDS CARESSING MY BREAST, MY WHOLE BODY, HIS WHISPERS, HIS LUSTFUL KISSES...

IT MUST HAVE BEEN TOO COLD, CAUSE HE GOT FROZEN IN SOME OTHER ZONE, ANOTHER REALM...MY LION'S MIND WAS IN A CAGE ON ITS OWN AND HE LEFT ME ALL ALONE, ALONE IN MY THOUGHTS REMINISCING ON WHAT WAS, IN THE BEGINNING; HOW REAL IT WAS, HOW I WAS JONESING MIND, BODY, AND SOUL...HOW HE WOULD ENGULF ME WITH ATTENTION AND AFFECTION...WHAT TO DO?!

I THOUGHT I HAD A FRIEND, A CONFIDANT WHO NEVER HAD TO FRONT, I THOUGHT IT WAS REAL BECAUSE OF THE WAY HE MADE ME FEEL WAS UNREAL...MY LION; YOU AIN'T FROM ZION, YOU FROM THE WOMB LIKE THE REST OF THEM GOONS...YOU LEFT ME IN THE COLD, NAKED FROM HEAD TO TOE, YOU HAD YOUR WAY, THEN WENT A STRAY...

I HAD ONLY ONE FEAR, AND THAT WAS MY TEARS, MY EMOTIONS WERE OVERFLOWING AND DIDN'T LET IT BE KNOWN, COULDN'T LET HIM SEE THE FROWN, FOR I AM A EMPRESS AND I WEAR THE CROWN...I HAVE RISEN ONCE

MORE AND I DON'T INTEND TO FALL, IT WAS JUST TOO COLD, THAT'S ALL...

# The Date

I was on a dinner date the other night…

Then he whispered and said; I wanna taste that vanilla caramel cream I see in my sight, before I can dive into the main course…I must satisfy the sweetness my taste buds must endure…whispers continued; hey sweetness it's your body I need to explore so I can devour you from head to toe or do I start in the middle where that vanilla, caramel cream settles…

He was thuggish, but not the way he spoke, he couldn't say; Nana, I wanna eat yuh pork!

# HUMBLE YU SELF (DUB POETRY)

YU NEED FI HUMBLE YU SELF...YU TOO MUCH INNA DI HYPE AND LOSE ALL YU STRIPE, DON'T YU KNOW WHAT IS RIGHT? MI SEH FI HUMBLE YU SELF...

MI SEH MI GIT UP INNA DI MORN, AN MI STILL DI A YAWN, MI NYAM SOME FOOD AND IT SOOD DI MOOD, MI SEH FI HUMBLE YU SELF...

MI GOH DUNG AH RIVAH FI CATCH TWO FISH, FI MI MAIN DISH, READ A PSALM AND BLOW MI CHALIS, HOL A HUMBLE THOUGHT AND GET A QUIK LIFT...WEN MI TEK A PRIPS, NOH CHRIS AND GLADIS A HOL A BIG KISS AN A REMINISCE...BUT A COULDAH WAH DIS, NOH DI SAME CHRIS WEH DEH WID JANIS! HIM NEED FI HUMBLE HIMSELF...

THEN MI TEK A STACK, NOH DI ONE JACK A GA LONG LACKA ACROBAT...A CLIMB DI TREE LACKA DAMN LITTLE RAT, DEN WEN MI TEK A STACK HIM DROP BRAP, LACKA RAT BAT AND BROK UP HIM BACK!...HIM NEED FI HUMBLE HIMSELF...

LOOK PON LUKE INNA CRIS BALLY BOOT AN VERSACE SUIT, A GOH LIK HIM CUTE, A WAH HAPEN TO DI FRUIT! HIM NEED FI HUMBLE HIMSELF...WAH HAPEN TO BUSH A BARE WAR HIM A PUSH, LOCK UP SADAM AN A HIM A MAD MAN! HIM NEED FI HUMBLE HIMSELF...

MI GIT UP INNA DE MORN AN MI ROOF IT GONE, WEN MI TEK A STACK NOH DI ONE IVAN! OH WAT A TING KILL OFF MI BRETHREN, MI SI ZING A FLY AN DEM NOH AV NO WING…LOOK LIKE HIM CUM FI WIPE OUT SOME SIN, OH WAT A TING…HIM NEED FI HUMBLE HIMSELF…

BLESSED IS THE MEEK, BLESSED IS MILD…ALWAYS BE HUMBLE, EVEN WITH A SMILE…

# THERAPY

DO YOU WANT ME TO BE YOUR PSYCHIATRIST OR JUST YOUR MENTAL THERAPIST...I WANT TO GET IN YOUR MIND AND LET YOU UNWIND...

I WANT TO TELL WHAT YOU'RE THINKING WHEN IT COMES TO ME, AND AT THIS TIME YOU ARE STARTING TO UNDRESS ME WITH YOUR MIND...DID YOU SEE THE WARNING SIGN? I DON'T THINK I CAN HELP YOU IF YOU GET TOO INCLINED, SO SIT BACK AND ENJOY THIS TIME AS I HYPNOTIZE YOU WITH THESE PREROGATIVE LINES...

YOU'RE NOT SURE JUST WHERE TO BEING, APPETIZERS ARE NORMALLY THE FIRST THING, AND THEN YOU DIVE IN...YOU HAVE DECIDED TO START BELOW THE BELLY RING, YOU WANT TO HAVE ME LIKE AN ACROBAT THAT CAN TWIST INTO ANYTHING, ANY DIMENSION YOU CAN SCRIPT IN YOUR MIND WHILE YOU UNWIND...STRAWBERRY AND CHOCOLATE SYRUP IS TO YOUR DELITE, AS YOU DEVOUR ME WITH ALL YOUR MIGHT...MY BODY TREMORS AS I EXPLODE, THEN YOU JOINED ME, SO THE STORY WAS TOLD...YOU WILL BE MY LION FOR I AM YOUR PREY WITH YOUR LONG MANE FILLED WITH WISDOM TO DIRECT ME YOUR WAY...

MY PRINCE, I AM YOUR EMPRESS, THAT I MUST SAY...NOW IT'S TIME TO WAKE FROM YOUR DISMAY, FOR IT WAS ONLY A DREAM I FAKED...IT'S THE END OF YOUR THERAPY AS YOU CAN SEE...IT WAS QUITE THE PLEASURE TO GET IN YOUR MOST PRIZED TREASURE!

# He…who?

I FELT A SUDDEN RUSH WHEN HIS BIG BROWN EYES TOUCHED MY CARAMEL SKIN, WHEN I IMAGINE EVERYTHING, MY NIPPLES ERECT AS HE BLOWS WHISPERS TO THE BACK OF MY NECK…

I ENGULFED HIS LUST WHEN OUR LOCKS TOUCH. I BECOME WEAK WHEN HE GETS ON HIS KNEES, HE LOOKED UP AT ME AND CALLED ME HIS QUEEN…WHEN HE EMBRACES ME I GO AFLOAT, "DOWN THE RIVER NILE WAS MY DESIRE"…MY JABARI, "BRAVE ONE" IN SWAHILI, MAKES ME MELT WITH HIS SMILE THAT'S SO FIERY, HIS SMILE OF SINCERITY, I NEED NOT DESPAIR….FOR HE IS MY CALM AFTER THE STORM, HE IS THE LION THAT KEEPS HIS LIONESS UNDER HIS ARMS….

I AM HIS EMPRESS, AND JAH KNOW, I'M BLESSED!

# INFINITY

INFINITY AND BEYOND WAS MY DESTINATION….AS I WALK
THROUGH THE VALLEY OF THE SHADOWS OF
EXCITEMENT, I FEARED HIS TONGUE AS HE WALKED
THROUGH THE VALLEYS OF RIPE FRUITS FRESHLY
SQUEEZED JUICES

# Definition of Love

Love is a passion, an emotion we all try to embrace when dignity has left us; we feel disgrace…mercy, mercy, why must you haste…

You see, you can be my banana, I be your split while you put your tongue on my clit…

You see, tonight it's all about deserts, and I'm gonna teach you to flirt, then I'm gonna let you know what a woman's worth, while we embrace and my tongue touches your immaculate places…these will be memories that can't be erased…we will do this at your pace, no I don't intend to race, you will be crying for the mercy of grace when I sit on your face…

# POETRY IS…

POETRY IS…..THE WAY HE SMILES, THE WAY HE LOOKS ME IN THE EYES AND SAYS; BABY BE MINE…

POETRY IS…..THE WAY HE CARESSES EVERY DEFINED SHAPE OF MY BODY…WHEN HE GETS IN MY MIND, BECAUSE I ALLOW HIM FROM TIME TO TIME…

POETRY IS…..HIS KISS THAT ALWAYS LEAVES ME TO REMINISCE OF THE WONDERS HE DOES WITH HIS LIPS…POETRY IS THE VERY BREATH HE BREATHES FROM HIS BODY…

POETRY IS…..COMPOSURE THAT I LOSE WHEN HE EMBRACES ME IN HIS SOMEWHAT STRONG ARMS, HE IS NOT A MUSCLE MAN, BUT ENOUGH TO LIFT ME TO THE LIMIT…

POETRY IS…..WHAT YOU PORTRAY IT TO BE; YOU CAN TAKE ONE GENDER, HE OR SHE, AND MAKE IT INTO AN EROTIC MYSTERY…

POETRY IS…..TO ME, BEING FREE AND THE FREEDOM TO BE… (In love as you can see)

# THE INSTRUMENTS…

I FELT LIKE THE SWEET SOUND OF THE SAXOPHONE BLOWING IN THE WIND, DRIFTING FROM ONE WORLD TO THE NEXT, SHOULD IT BE HIM OR HER?...

I AM TRAPPED WITHIN, LIKE A CELIBATE CAT IN HEAT, OH SWEET IT IS WHEN THE GUITARIST STRUMS AND STROKES HIS STRINGS, WITH EVERY MELODY MY BODY SINGS…

WHEN THE DRUMMER DRUMS ON THESE ASS-ETS, THE RHYTHM ENGULFS ME WITH EVERY BEAT, OH MY BODY IN HEAT! MADE ME MELT INTO AN OCEAN OF EXCITEMENT I COULD NOT DEFEAT…

MY BODY PULSATES LIKE THE HARMONY THE PIANIST PLAYED…OUR HEARTS IN UNISON SOUNDING LIKE THE SYMPHONY FROM A BROADWAY MUSICAL.RHYTHMICALLY, OUR BODIES COLLIDED CAUSING AN EXPLOSION WITH A DOMINO REACTION…SENDING VIBRATIONS OF MUSICAL NOTES, "DO, RE, MI, FA, SOL, LA, TI, DO". DOWN MY SPINE, CHIMES RESONATE FROM THE IVORY OF OUR SMILES…WHISPERS OF MELODIES LUMINATES THE SKY, SHIT I WAS HIGH….HIGH ON A MUSICAL VIBE.

# SMILE…

COME OVER HERE LET ME SPEAK TO YOU FOR A WHILE…

IT WOULD BE NICE TO SEE YOU, THAT SMILE AND THOSE BEAUTIFUL PEARLS YOU CALL TEETH, THE QUIVERING OF YOUR LIPS WHEN WE KISS…

YOUR EYES HOW THEY PENETRATE ME WHEN WE TOUCH, OH WHAT GLORIOUS LUST…WHEN THAT SMILE IGNITES ME TO HIGH, I FEEL LIKE A SAXOPHONE BLOWING IN THE WIND, MELODIES FROM DEEP WITHIN, OH SMILE AWHILE…

CLOSE YOUR EYES, LET ME TAKE YOU SOMEWHERE, I'M GONNA HAVE YOU MESMERIZED, REMINISCING ON THESE THIGHS, MANY WILL DESPISE…AND WITH THOSE LIPS ON THESE TITS, MAKES ME FANTASIZE ABOUT IT, THE GENTLENESS WITH EVERY TOUCH, MAKES ME WANT IT ROUGH, DON'T PLAY TOUGH…

COME OVER HERE, MY INSIDES NEED TO FEEL THE HARDNESS OF YOUR MANLY ANATOMY; I KNOW IT WON'T BRING ME SADNESS, BUT STRAIGHT MADNESS, THAT WILL LEAVE ME SMILING FOR A LONG WHILE…

# Composure…

HE FLATTERED ME WITH HIS WORDS, AND PENETRATED ME WITH HIS EYES AS HIS FINGERS CARESSED MY LIPS TO NO RETURN, THE LIPS OF MOTHER EARTH THAT BROUGHT FORTH 3 LIVES…THE WHISPERS DRIVES ME INSANE…

LOSING MYSELF, I MUST SUSTAIN…. COMPOSURE IS MY ONLY CLAIM…

# THE LETTER...

HELLO MY DEAR FRIEND, MY INFATUATION...

HOPE YOUR MIND IS AT PEACE WHEN YOU READ THROUGH THESE FEW LINES...YOU SEE, THERE IS A NEED DEEP INSIDE ME, AND THAT'S TO BE WITH YOU EVERY WAKING MOMENT...

THERE IS SO MUCH I CRAVE ABOUT YOU, PLEASE BELIEVE WHEN I SAY THE SOUND OF YOUR VOICE LEAVES ME BREATHLESS, MAKES ME SMILE EVEN WHEN I CRY...

I DON'T KNOW WHAT IT IS ABOUT YOU THAT'S LEFT ME SO INFATUATED WITH YOU, MAYBE IT'S THAT DAMN SMILE, OR MAYBE IT'S THAT DAMN LAUGH THAT'S SO UNIQUE IT LEAVES ME WET, YEARNING TO HOLD YOU...YES, OUR RELATIONSHIP IS VERY IMPORTANT TO ME....

YOU SEE, I NEED YOU INSIDE MY LUST-TUROUS MIND....ABOUT TO EXPLODE WITH JUST THE THOUGHT OF YOU TELLING ME WHAT TO DO, AM I WRONG TO FEEL THIS WAY...YOU OKAY WITH ME SHARING MY INFATUATION, DO YOU WANNA PLAY?...WE ONLY A LETTER AWAY...

P.S.

TO BE CONTINUED...

# LIFE and RELATIONS

FUCK! You think you find happiness and it's another dead end to sadness, what's all this madness!

This anger I can't express, too much stress! Life and Relations…

DAMN IT! I need to stick to me, not the opposite being, Life…why so many complications to being happy, to be free…It's more painful than giving birth, you push and it's over in a matter of days, hours, sometimes weeks, but relations…is nonetheless continuous pain, pain you cannot find words to explain…you on a high for a few days, engulfing each other's inhabitations: pass, present and future…conversations of planting a seed for us to nurture, a life, what kinda relation, will only be another broken limb for that rock-a-bye baby seed! Gimme some weed! So I can meditate on a high, so I can reminisce on what was before da bliss clouded over my heart causing my mental state to depart…

What da FUCK! Are you gonna be alive and miserable or alive and happy? LIFE is too short!

LIFE and RELATIONS!

# TIME

I love you in a place where there is no "time"

In my heart there will always be a place for you and I…There we worry not of "time" for all our lives…

In my dreams, always your silhouette lingers in the sky…For everywhere I am you will always be, the epitome of my memories…

Life is what we make it, "time" always needing to face it…I've been loving you in my heart, in my mind, seems like an eternity only with "time"…

What do we do when we have now reached the pinnacle that has caused our juices to collide...Do we refrain from pride?…There is just no "time"…

Decisions we've made throughout the years, have dissipated our mental state…

But when destiny materializes, "time" only becomes a figment of our imagination, in disguise…

# LAUGHTER

WHAT IS LIFE WITHOUT LAUGHTER?

WITH LAUGHTER, EVEN WHEN YOU'RE LOSING, YOU'RE WINNING WITH JOY OF LIFE…

LAUGHTER, THE LAUGHTER THAT MAKES THE JOYOUS TEARS FALL FROM THE CORNER OF YOUR EYES…

LAUGHTER THAT MAKES YOU GRAB THE MIDDLE PASSAGE BETWEEN YOUR THIGHS, YOU OR I…

LAUGHTER THAT MAKES YOU STOMP YOUR FEET, CLAPPING YOUR HANDS TO THE SOUND OF THE BEAT, EVEN SOMETIMES ON THE HARD CONCRETE, NOT REALIZING THE HURT UNTIL YOU THROW YOUR HANDS UP, BEGGING PLEASE!!...

LAUGHTER, SLAPPING THE BACK OF A FRIEND JOYFULLY, SENDING THEM FLYING TO OTHER SIDE OF THE ROOM…

LAUGHTER, LIKE FRESH AIR HARMONIZING TO THE TRUTH, THE MELODIES OF DIFFERENT TONES SERENADING OUR SOULS…

LAUGHTER HAS A CERTAIN WAY OF REJUVENATING THE MIND TAKING YOU BACK SOMEWHERE IN TIME, MAYBE CLOUD NINE…LISTENING TO A JAM THAT WAS OH SO DIVINE, MAYBE 79…

LAUGHTER, NATURAL HEALING FOR OUR SOULS, PASS IT ON AND GAIN LOTS MORE…

# RHYMES, RAP and DO WOP

DO DAT ORIGINAL RAP…

DO DAT ORIGINAL RAP…

DO DAT ORIGINAL RAP…

I'M NOT A RAPPA BUT I CAN TALKA…

I'M NOT A RAPPA BUT I CAN TALKA…SPIT TWO RHYMES AND MAKE YA SAY WHOA…SPIT TWO RHYMES AND MAKE YA SAY; WHOA!

DO DAT ORIGINAL RAP…

DO DAT ORIGINAL RAP…

DO DAT ORIGINAL RAP…

DO DAT ORIGINAL RAP…

NANA BE RHYMING POETICALLY CLIMBING ON THE RIGHT TIMING…BOOM BAP, DA ORIGINAL; RAP!

# STRENGTH

DON'T LET MY STRENGTH INTIMIDATE YOU, LET IT STRENGTHEN YOU…

DON'T LET MY STRENGTH CLOUD YOUR SKIES, LET MY STRENGTH ILLUMINATE AND GUIDE…

DON'T LET MY STRENGTH DISCOURAGE YOU FROM FINDING YOUR OWN STRENGTH WITHIN, LET MY STRENGTH MOTIVATE YOU TO STRIVE ENGAGING YOU IN POSITIVE ONLY VIBES, NOT ONCE, TWICE, BUT ALL THE TIMES…

MY STRENGTH…

# My Journey

My journey has taken me through years of knowledge gained and knowledge shared…

My journey has brought me through many battles, many elements, many victories, pain…

My journey has taken me through the shadows of death, yet I fear no evil, for jah is always with me…

My journey has taken me through motherhood, blessed with 3 other souls that I continuously need to mold and keep illuminated with unconditional love…even after the light has gone out, there will never be a doubt…

# Fighting The Feeling

Is it greed, is it lust, is it envy…is it a must?

I look at you and I see that shoe I just had to have, you know the one with the diamond tip…yet I want no more, let me get out the store…fighting the feeling once more…

I see that jean that fits my every, curve all so sweet…yet I want no more…fighting the feeling, oh let me go to sleep

I see a man I wanna always chill with, laugh talk even play tag with, a little kiss, a touch, maybe a feel….but he is spoken for so it won't be real…fighting the feeling is all I can say…sigh; "real" should come naturally, not from play…

I see that sports car, you know the one without the top, nice bright color to brighten the spot, a few joy rides with OPP, but fight the feeling is all that's left for me…

I see that winner for planting a seed, in my garden where brilliant flowers will be reaped…yet my garden is at rest, with jah it's all blessed, he has given 3 that has bloomed and continues to flourish with glee…I know with your energy it will no longer suppress, fighting the feeling cause us such stress, keeping it real is always best…

We fighting the feeling all through life, battling lust, envy and greed, don't forget about pride…with humbling composure you just might succeed…might strive

Continue fighting the feeling as you please, our eyes will always lead us to deceive…

FIGHTING THE FEELING…

# BREATHING THOUGHTS

My brain is screaming for help, my body aches, my heart continues to beat to every breath that was caressing my thoughts…my breast danced to the rhythm of the bass coming from his chest, I'm a mess…no stress! I inhaled his breath…his thoughts read out;…

"Now that I'm inside I can have my way, thanks for the invite…I'm gladly accepting your invitation as you breathe deeper, the elements of my essence mesh with your senses, my cells conversing with your cells, every time you inhale…keep breathing" (E.Str8)

I got wet…oh my thoughts has brought me….ah, maybe his breath has brought me to ecstasy, me breathing him has turned me into a fiend…oh my mind I have sucked him in double time, all 6, plus 2 deep, and 3 wide…my mind; how captivating…my thoughts or is it my imagination?…

"While you in this transformation, let me tame your imagination; this is eradication of your past relations…let me give you a translation…baby I'm your conscience, let me be your guide, no brakes with E, you're safe, relax and take this spiritual ride"…just breathe… (E.Str8)

I swear telepathy kicked in, this was more than mental stimulation…our juices collided, our hearts were in gyration…oh what a sensation, is this really my imagination…

"What you imagine is actually your passion, the way your body's reacting is just a reaction like it can't believe that this is really happening…Caption this; the feeling is real when I'm filling your chambers with real wind…every time you exhale you're really sexually healing"…(E.Str8)

His breath had me crawling the ceiling, he was fucking me telepathically while he was breathing…mentally fucking me while sleep was at its prime, so divine…

# Thoughts…

What do we do now, where do we go from here, do I disappear?…

Will the search continue for who, when, where…flying to all these different hemispheres, the life I fear to wear, need not compare?…

What is it we seek?...

We were high on life, on some trees, we were like feens…we were hookah blowing, Jack sipping, honey licking, sweat dripping high…wet dreams between the sheets high on life, kinda high…

# More Thoughts…

My soul is bewildered, my strength is sustained, my body is weak my brain in pain…sanity is my claim

The energy that surrounds me, I wish not to maintain…killing me softly resounds in my brain, I might as well be dead, may I proclaim…

Our love for money has weakened our souls, condemned our hearts and corrupted our thoughts…

# SPOKEN

ACTION SPEAK LOUDER THAN WORDS…THE WORDS PROJECTED BY YOUR VOICE BOX, WORDS SPOKEN OUT IN THE UNIVERSE; LET ME QUENCH YOUR THIRST!

JUDGE ME NOT BY THE WORDS I HAVE SPOKEN FOR THEY ARE MANY, BUT JUDGE ME BY ACTIONS FOR THEY ARE FEW…

SPOKEN WORDS, BROKEN SO MANY TIMES, EVAPORATES WITH WISDOM AS WE DECLINE…THEY SAY STICKS AND STONES CAN BREAK YOU, BUT YOUR WORDS DON'T HURT…LIE

ARE YOU NOT BROKEN FROM WORDS 'SPOKEN'….THESE BROKEN WORDS SPOKEN SO MANY TIMES CREATING ILLUSIONS SO DEFINED, CONFUSING THE MIND…

# TATTOOS

MEMORIES THAT STAINS THE LIPS, LEAVING MANY
TATTOOS ON MY BRAIN...

DON'T KNOW BOUT TOMORROW; JUST LIVE FROM DAY TO
DAY WITH MEMORIES OF YESTERDAY, TOMORROW AND
TODAY...

ECHOES OF TATTOOS, HAUNTING MELODIES PLAY OVER
AND OVER AGAIN...

SHADOWS, SILHOUETTES, REMNANTS OF YESTERDAY
STIMULATING MY MIND, MY THOUGHTS SEXUALLY
INCLINED; ECLECTICALLY FUCKING THE WORDS
PROJECTING FROM MY MIND...

# "KNOCK KNOCK"

KNOCK KNOCK…JONESING FOR SOME VERBAL STIMULATION, MENTAL PENETRATION…WHEN LOVE COMES KNOCKING, WILL IT BE THE BREATH HE BREATHES, THE ECHOES OF HIS HEART INSYNC WITH OUR INTELLECTUAL VIBRATION…SWEET SENSATION?

WHEN LOVE COMES KNOCKING HOW WILL I KNOW?...HOW WILL YOU KNOW? WILL IT BE HIS TOUCH?…MAYBE THE VERY ESSENCE OF HIS BEING

WHEN LOVE COMES KNOWING, HOW WILL YOU KNOW…BEEN DOWN THIS ROAD BEFORE; WILL IT BE THE WORDS HE SPEAKS OR WILL IT BE JUST IN MY MIND…MIND IN GREAT DISTRESS, ILLUSIONS AT ITS BEST

WHEN LOVE COMES KNOCKING, HOW WILL I KNOW WHAT WILL BE THE BEST, MY HEART'S A MESS…SILHOUETTE ON THE WALL LOOKED LIKE YOU, THEN REALIZED IT WAS ONLY THE SHADOWS IN MY MIND LINGERING FROM TIME TO TIME, DELUSIONAL IS MORE OPTIONAL…

WHEN LOVE COMES KNOCKING, WILL IT BE AN INTELLECTUAL STIMULATION, MAYBE A VERBAL VIBRATION…"KNOCK KNOCK"…MAYBE JUST A SIMPLE EYE CONTACT…

# GIVE BIRTH

MOTHER EARTH CRIES GIVING BIRTH TO HUMANITY, TO hypocrisy, social illusions leaving you delusional-ly…zombie nation beyond the imagination…

MOTHER EARTH CONTINUES GIVING BIRTH TO A NEW GENERATION OF CLONES, GMOs,…CYCLONES, WORLD WINDS DISTURBING HER CYCLE…MIND, BODY, EARTH; CONFUSING US FROM BIRTH, DEEPLY SHE HURTS, ERUPTIONS OF ORGASMIC EXPLOSIONS….DESTRUCTION! OSMOSIS EMBODIES HER EVERY "ATOM" A "MATTER"-OF-FACT, HER VERY BEING…MOTHER EARTH, HER WOMB SO JADED, NATIONS LEFT WITH CONTRITE SPIRITS AND NAKED MIND…MANKINDS, MOTHER EARTH SO DIVINE…

# More Thoughts…

Calling Mommy's phone, leave a message after the tone…"I know you might be sleeping, but just wondering how you keeping…

I constantly feel the urge to hear your voice, to hear you tell me; "don't cry babe"….then I would rest my head on your chest, my favorite place to be…

# Youngin…

Youngin don't be shy, can your young mind move an empress like I?…

Take a walk with me in the hills by and by…I wanna teach you a little sum thing bout Jah Rastafari….come on baby don't sigh, let me teach how to treat an empress in jah eyes…

Youngin you said you been in the streets from youth was by your side and knows what it takes to make a woman not cry, know what to do to keep her satisfied…but do you know what this empress desires?...

Don't wait to hear for I won't tell you, you know the streets so I may sound like a fool; tell me if you're ready to be schooled…if you're ready to learn some of my golden rules…

You might be optimistic for a youngin you see, for most youngins don't know their destiny, don't know their future is always a priority…

# ROOTS...

Galvanized from the Roots....Clothed with shame....
Dishonored to my demise....

Galvanized from the Roots...Confused at their rejoice...No, I am
not bulletproof...

Galvanized from the Roots...
Backbone strength curved out of iron, copper tone...oh don't let
me take you to that zone....
Blessed with three hearts beats, only my own, truly known...

Galvanized from the Roots...
By the grace of God, I will be magnified and pacified with
faith...who said this life was a disgrace, anything black is waste, u
better know your place...

Galvanized you, Galvanized me....Galvanized from the Roots, my
melanin, my truth...

# "THANK YOU"

Dear God,

I just wanted to say; Thank You...

Thank You for putting me in my father's sperm bank, Thank You for picking me to be placed in the warm sac of Mother Earth's incubator...whom you have taken back into your bosoms to join your nation of guardian angels...

Thank You for the atoms, the matters, and the molecules that have created me....molecules that bloomed into a flower fragile as a rose, one petal at a time, but resilient as an orchid...

Thank You for "LIFE"...
Living under the supremacy of the unknown...Life is what you make it, your story, your journey...only God knows...

Thank You God for staying manifested in my Soul...so mlack, so pure, my melanin I adore....

Thank You GOD!....saying it out LOUD!!...don't be astound because I'm proud to the bone...

Thank You for the wisdom of humility that will set me free...

Thank You God!!....For me!

# COUNTING...

Been a matter of TIME for many years, just enough to capture every MOMENT within those times....memorable, and moments you don't wish to give a chance taking up space in your cranium, all you can do is sit and hum to the sweet melody of your heart, beats sounding like the ticking of a clock...counting; will time be by our side, or against us, they say only time will tell, but is it really the time or is it the moment....

Or is it the moment we "will" it to be...

# STROKE...

With every stroke, I lay awake reminiscing on what we had; create...was it a mistake to fall in deep with someone that wasn't free to be?...

With every stroke, I feel my heart pulsate...bringing me to an abnormal state, do I masturbate, it was great never fake...

With every stroke, his fingers caress, I lose my breath, about to melt...dripping wet, stroke after stroke, waiting to explode...

With every stroke time stands still, shadows and silhouettes elope, creating a kaleidoscope of orgasmic pleasure, how do we measure?...

With every stroke of my cheeks, I feel you deep within me, energy unknown...and there I was alone, awake in my dream...so I scream

# BEAUTIFUL

No better being than the being that you are...Beautiful by far

Impairment may cloud your vision....but your beauty will always prevail...illuminating your path as the bright of day...

Mobility may shorten your steps, but who was counting anyways....diminished with age and still beautiful with style and grace...

Abused from an early age, child, youth, teenage...oh what disgrace the abuse you have faced...ugly has no place

Living in fear because of the echoes in your heart saying; you won't amount to nothing, you are just a fault

Suffocated by doubt, depression has shortened your breath, suppressing your growth...wait on the Lord; but be of good courage...beautification of your soul is his promise...

Rape not justified, who made the rules a man or a guy, it is all a lie, wife, daughter, sister...even I; you are Beautiful, just let it shine...

Abandoned treasures in disguise, earthen vessels from realms far and wide; cast down, yet not destroyed; perplexed without despair, as the beauty in you will always prevail...Be free

# And more thoughts…

The silhouette of his manhood lingers in my head....his every stroke, his every tread...

The very essence of his being, Lord I'm a feen...wouldn't mind being his queen...

# Potential…

This potential is at it....he is already having issues with my outspokenness...

This potential is at it....really not my type, maybe just the hype...

This potential is at it!...am I not to speak, better to be meek....truth is uttered, his defense is; you talk too much....not particularly pleased; pleasure from this potential is yet to be discovered...

This potential is at it....OMG, why can I not have the freedom to be, freedom to speak, the freedom to clarity...

This potential is pathetic…me give empathy, hell no! Not even for a minute….

# LOVE IS DEAD...

Love is Dead...
Love was a neighbor from emotion land...
Love had a family; Infatuation, Lust, Envy and Deceit...

Love is Dead...
Love and Infatuation always confuse everyone, how to
differentiate often leads to mistakes; birth from Mother Earth's
emotions within... Eluted from the atoms, matters, the molecules
of lust...
Lust, was the brotha who just never gets enough, always bringing
Love into his equation, a major sensation that doesn't add up...

Love is Dead...
Deceit never fails, always the one smiling, while silently ripping
you apart, often when Love is away, Deceit will come out to
play...

# FRIGHT or FLIGHT

Too much distraction, that's only half the fraction, no mental satis-fraction…

Insta, Facebook, What's App, Twitter…Who wanna play? The World Wide Web navigating your life, how it ends, what's the price…

Messages subliminally, metaphors' of broken tones, who knows when this series will come to an end…there will be another episode of 'the days of our life"

Another political Fright or Flight…nowhere to hide, how do we fight this political warfare, Chem-Trails polluting and muting our air, too much fear in the atmosphere…

World-Demic, Pandemic, Plan-Demic, Poli-Tricks, Systemic, Bio-Genics…world shut down, everyone a clown, puppets on a string…

# Cherry on Top

Cherry lips open wide, kissing, licking, sucking, fucking…tongue deep penetration

An energy engulf me, sending me adrift in an ocean unknown….drip drip dripping wet

Cherry lips so tasty, desert on its own…sometimes creamy whipped, even honey dipped, caramel glazed that leaves a smile on your face…even plain for the sugar free feens in a daze…finger licking wet, daze…

Kisses turn to purple as my breath begins to dissipate, my body begins to pulsate…CPR resounds…yes, cock pussy resuscitation was my tone

Cherry lips tasting the juices of life, fingers deep, pleasures erupt…cherry lips solidify with every kiss between my thighs…I am satisfied!

# Thoughts…

Let's shine a light for all the Mothers that have perished…In our hearts they will always be cherished…Memories untold that illuminates the soul…

# Thoughts continue…

KISSING MY BODY LIKE THE MORNING SUN, AS THE RAYS ENERGIZE MY SOUL,

LIPS WET LIKE THE DEW SITTING IN A HONEYSUCKLE, BIRDS AND THE BEES

HUMMING SWEET NOTHINGS, DAYDREAMING WITH EYES WIDE OPEN,

ROOFTOP ECHOS AS THE RAIN DROPS DID SOME DRUMMING, MOSQUITOES

ZIPPING BY TRYING TO HARMONIZE THEIR NOTES ON A HIGH…MY WHOLE

BEING…SOLACE WAS MY STATE, IN A SPACE WHERE SADNESS HAD NO

PLACE…

# MORE THAN…

More Than Friends, yet to be determined what it is you're seeking?…

You say; More Than Friends was what you was thinking, quenching your thirst is your inclination…more than friends with every nation, stress or satisfaction…stop faking

More Than Friends, no one in control, leaving room to explore and explore…I'm gonna say more, but a free style living is what you require, more than friends is really your desire…needing to put out that fire

More than friends is just your desire, while annulment will be void, shit expired!

More than friends, some kind of entrapment…while stealing my soul, my chakras…total body shut down…equilibrium unsteady, from your crown to your root…now you're mute

You say; More Than Friends, sounds like a good beginning, waiting on the "friendship" to evolve before the "more" kicks into another explore, another score, then walk out the door…more than you know

# Thinking…

Destin we are, near and far, searching for that one true star…

Through the clouds, infinity and beyond, that one true star will be found…

# Thoughts of…

I am the pinnacle of your being, the very breath you breathe, the blood running through your veins, the cells that multiply you into your prime, time after time…

I am mother earth, I give birth to life…to the continued strive, staying alive, and staying magnified…

I am…

# "LIFE"

Life is memories filled of disappointments, fuljoyment, sadness, laughter…filled with what you make it…ice cream truck sounds its melody as it comes around the corner…echoes of happy children running in the streets…when you last your virginity, skipping school, when you first conceived…single mother Life, married Life…fuck then you divorce, kind of Life…

D – DIVIDED

I – INDIVIDUALIZED

V – VICTIMIZED

O – OFFENDED

R – REFUSED

C – CANCELLED

E – EVICTED

Life is a cycle, so be sure to recycle goodness, Godliness, keeping the heart clean, counting your blessings in all your dreams…

Life is what you make it, who you make be a part of it…whose Life is it? Yours? His? Theirs?

Only you can navigate your own destiny, your Life…

# MAMA BACK BONE…

Looking at the reflections of my mind, wish I could erase all the corruption it entails…if I can only let go of the hatred that has captured my fears, my wells are dry, no tears will appear, nothing to compensate…

My memoirs…memoirs of a Rasta woman…I'm like a lioness in a cage mentally pacing back and forth…wanting to break free from myself, from memories that have taken residency in my mind, not allowing me to strive…

I remember when I was five, it was a tenement yard of about twenty-five…oh what ah life

Mama would work till late at night, Papa did the same, affi goh dung a garage wait till late, boat a run, chalice a bun, mi fada a chant pon a kette drum…Jah Jah bless, Jah Jah bless…don't you love how it sounds….and he chanted, and he chanted…mi chant back; mi agoh bless, mi agoh bless…for so it was told, give thanks fi Mama Back Bone…her and daddy would fight late at night, them work hard every day, underpaid like continued slaves, side piece to fill the space…

I remember that night when I was about nine, Mama screamed out and cried, err mada dead a foreign, and that's where it all began…left on my own to face the world without Mama Back Bone…

I remember hip hopping, break dancing, jumping and prancing…dancing on stage keeping a smile on my face, trying not to be a slave in this race…backflips, back-bone-slide, suicides…foreign life!

Mama BackBone set the tone…

# GENERATIONAL

GENERATIONAL CURSE, GENERATIONAL THIRST,
GENERATIONAL INDIFFERENCES…WHAT IS YOUR
WORTH?, GENERATIONAL STRENGTH, GOOD HEALTH,
GENETICS, DNA….SEARCHING FOR THE UNKNOWN,
TRYING TO UNSCRAMBLE WHAT'S LEFT OF THE PUZZLE,
LET THE PAST GO OF STORIES UNTOLD, GENERATIONAL
WHAT, WHO, WHEN, WHERE, GENERATIONAL
WEALTH…WHAT IS IT TO GAIN, WHO WILL NAME THE
CLAIM?MAYBE YOU WILL, MAYBE YOU WON'T, BE READY
TO EMBRACE WHAT IT UNFOLDS…GENERATIONAL
INDIFFERENCES, REMEMBER TO CROSS YOUR T's AND
DOT YOUR I's, OR WE MAY NEVER KNOW OUR BIRTH
RIGHT…KINGS AND QUEENS IN THE STREETS, LIVING LIKE
THIEVES…HOW WILL WE KNOW OUR GENETICS WERE
STOLEN, WHEN WE REALLY ALL JUST BROKEN? GENETIC
CHAIN MISPLACED…INDIGENOUS TO THE BONE, THEN
ADD SOME MELANIN TO SOOTH THE TONE…PROCREATE,
WHO TO CLAIM, GENERATIONAL DISMAY, GENERATIONAL
INDIFFERENCES…STILL MAKING THE LIST

# SLEEPING

Woke up with you on my mind…don't know what the future holds, but do hope to see you again one day soon…in real time for sure, as the stories in that book of Life unfolds, doors open doors close, on a journey of the unknown, not knowing day from night no more…

Mind locked in solitary confinement, bars shut tight, not a window in sight…you and I, undefined…

Woke up with you on my mind, didn't think you would leave me behind…Sipping a little wine, antiquated images takes me back in time, where we been down this road before, could it be a Déjà vu...let me check my view

You see, I'm trying to let go of you, memories sticking like crazy glue, waking emotions never knew existed…how do I fix this?…

Woke up with you on my mind…counting the time, unpredicted, so is our life…

# THORNS…

It's said; "that without sacrifice there will be no victory" …
(King Arthur).

See, it was like trying to do back strokes downstream…how can
two thorns connect? Let's do the math, recalculate,
recalibrate…make no mistake, cause the road to hell is paved
with good intentions, deception! Show me loyalty in your actions,
words are never a satisfaction, only half of the fraction…

How can two thorns connect, will sure be a bloody mess…they
say opposite attracts, two of the same causes flames, could be in
a negative or positive way…what you portray

# Little Thought…

When I was drowning, he was my anchor, yet I pondered…

Was drowning a better option…

Maybe just some mental satisfaction…

# Thoughts…

Living like a hermit in my own head…captured in my thoughts, meditative state was my decline, not able to differentiate between thoughts and reality, real time…

# Just Saying…

Lord, not sure what you're showing me yet, but do I jump, leap, run, prance, skip or just sit, sit and be humble?…"The meek shall inherit the land", I don't want that…the land, but bless me with that man, that one true King deserving this Queen, this Earthly being…

As humble as I may be, temptation, along with desires, at times tends to get the best of me…

Take the leap for God will guide me? But my memories suppress my mobility…

Do I take it, do I jump, leap, run, prance, skip?

A virtuous woman indeed I am, so my patience is never a plan…Waiting on the Lord and being of good courage, cause the Lord is the Earth and the goodness thereof…my courage, my strength is all I have, my patience, well that's a plus…

# Thoughts…

There is no price for having self-esteem…you can wear it, like you wear the skin you're in or fear it, fear that dominates you to having none!...

# HOPE…

Hope the sun is shining where-ever you are…

Hope the rays are kissing your skin, energizing your soul, body and mind, bringing Hope in your life, a smile in your heart…putting some joy into your feet…fanning your hands to the heat, with thoughts suffocated by self-doubt, wondering; "will there ever come change to my route?…Hoping for another day to come, when will you and the sun become one?, that even in the moonlight the sun will be shining in…

With hope, little faith, there is not much to anticipate…

www.ingramcontent.com/pod-product-compliance
Lightning Source LLC
LaVergne TN
LVHW021539080426
835509LV00019B/2729